M000314725

love letters to places...

anja mujic

Copyright © Anja Mujic, 2022
Published 2022 by The Book Reality Experience

ISBN: 978-1-922670-32-8 - Paperback 2nd Edition
ISBN: 978-1-922670-33-5 - EBook Edition

All rights reserved.

The right of Anja Mujic to be identified as author of this Work has been asserted by her
in accordance with sections 77 and 78 of the Copyright, De-signs and Patents Act 1988.

This book is a work of fiction and any resemblance to actual persons, living or dead, is
purely coincidental.

No part of this publication may be reproduced, stored in retrieval system, copied in any
form or by any means, electronic, mechanical, photocopying, recording or otherwise
transmitted without written permission from the publisher. You must not circulate this
book in any format.

for every time,

place,

and other...

i. unliving...

i found myself in the unliving. in the tip-toed dance that swept me as far across the bulbed fields of keukenhof and the fragrant sprigs of valensole as it did across the lines in the sand of my own life, drawn for lifetimes on end. in the shattering of golden chains and encrusted cages scattered across wastelands like kutná hora's ossein leftovers, eagerly awaiting to be collected and ceremonially dipped in fondue. in the surrender to every coaxing whisper and beckoning finger born of both the pulse within and the call without, an unknowing of being good for good's sake, an unseeing of sights seen behind infant eyelids ripped like bandaids just to be coated in sweetness and sneakily snuck back into place. left with a memoir of moments as fleeting as sahara snowflakes on skin and every sensation memorised of a dream, the unravelling of a tattered blueprint, once an instruction manual, soon a mere suggestion, cradled like santa ana quicksand between slippery fingertips. the fear thrown back as if it were a tonic for the ailment itself; an unquenchable thirst for every time, place and other. dreamscapes and dreamstates fuelled by unexpected treasures laying await in eagerly outstretched palms, those unseeming epicentres of the beauty truth so badly craves, howling in the face of every pair of devilish eyes and rose-watered hands that keep the living enslaved on seemingly emerald pastures. an entire life to be unlived and lived again, in just one breath. drenched in sweat and sweet nectar that flowed freely into the rivers of my blood. all the way until we became one. in the unliving.

amsterdam...

does naivety count as the punchline? cause i seemed even funnier
to the threatened swan and the hollow eyed, promises
feigned to dissolve every care and trouble away in her
dappled folds, like hypnotic melodies that sweetly swayed from
their butcher shop
windows adrip with hue, a honey'd land of promise renewed for
juvenile tongues a flicker
of light, a parting of lips, a crimson to engulf even the most
suffocated of slates
clean like a sharp inhale or the first crisp break of applause
for the end of an era
that had to be unlived so that i could go on living. lost
in a sea of wheels reminiscent
of novelty sized doorknobs reflecting the warped faces
of a hundred hysterically laughing horses
with pupils the envy of van gogh's and every other starry night
that glistened
like a thousand eager tendrils steadily creeping
towards that first crisp break of dawn...

twenty ten ft. coldplay and the hill sisters (tram 2)...

a few double turns occurred at the radial corner; one for the tram incessantly tracing the spine of its city like an unrelenting lover, two for the bag of bones riding it. both with a gut wrenching lull, and a silent, slow motion scream. both serenaded by songs titled to mark the occasion

(a sentiment seemingly apt at the time). threats to derail only brought me closer to the eye of the storm, calm as the most dangerous crimson emanating from around forbidden corners, a beginning and ending on one, as fresh as a first breath and as stale as a last. how was it that a glow, so salacious, was the only thing that could saturate such tender bitterness in such bitter tenderness? maybe once you (think you) know every tangible pleasure held in rococo stone and pounds of flesh, all that's left is what lays dormant beneath, beyond, within. that which only takes its encores for rounds of applause made not between greedily greased up palms but between the sun's bullet rays and the surface of the gouden bocht. contemplative moments shattered by reality and reflective handlebars (such trouble makers for the sights young curiosity seeks to devour). luxury not found in the thirty bed dorms reminiscent of limbs lost in bathroom games, but abounding faces anew that in an instant reflected my beneath, beyond and within better than any old ones pretending to. celebrated with me and by me.
by daylight and twilight.

- *it was a good time for a double turn...*

contiki catharsis (an ode to techno)...

2/4, 120bpm

Grey rain Melting slate
Rooftops Dipped in Solid Gold
Peach beer on Sweet tongues
Top bunk Bottoms up
Awkward hands fumbled inthe (dark)
Scenic windows Derailed tracks
Awkward silence noLooking back
Eastside shine Westside glow
Sunset view was Split-in-Two
Warm baths Rogue ghosts
Climbing Midnight LampPosts
Techno beats Jazzkey notes
greenFairy Tales and Doorways
Lined with Crossed Bones
some guy named... henry, acid kiss...
fingertips... all night bliss...
rosé skylines, tangled limbs
salt filled sea(side) bonesBroken in
Crescent moon shaped glacier lake
full Circle rainbow found its way

mountains sugared with wildflowerfields
but Still, thebushome Ends-in-Tears
Grey rain Melting slate
Rooftops Dipped in Solid Gold

neon pink heart (antwerp)...

do you remember standing beneath a neon pink heart, with your cupped hands collecting every unquenched thirst thus far, that spilled from your mouth and every wrinkled fold, that lined your pockets, palms, and passport?

the latitudes to be read, the inked scars to be acquired, the dreams to be memorised in curved brick motifs and curious prayers sung (but never for salvation), next to unsold trinkets collecting dust, taking up way too much space next to sonnets and soliloquies scrawled on rogue post-its,
next to those phone numbers you pretend you'll need again, and as many tales of myth and royalty as can be heard and retold just to prove your place?

do you remember every laboured breath, every weighted moment, the searing desire for nothing and everything, all at once, wishing the moment would brand you like the neon pink wire did antwerp's forget-me-not-sky, the envy of its presence in every place and time?

the oblivion to eviscerate every slumbered moment that didn't match the one placed on your sleeve for safekeeping, like a jewel pulled from the port's murkiest depths by the sun weathered hands reminding you not to lose it, or break it, or pull it out only on special occasions?
do you remember going on to some other time and place, like none of it happened, but suddenly dressed in this indulgent glow of presence, and no desire, to ever go back?

\-   *memories imprinted by presence*

two strangers in venice...

everyone has their own version
bound in leather, or silver halide emulsified to keep
in those faraway corners of the bottom drawer, still
i wonder if he'd remember it the way i do…
how we stumbled, drunk on stolen slumber, out that furnace of a
sleeper
into a dawn fire raging on a floating city not yet spoiled
by hoards throwing pebbles at rioting birds exploding
into sounds of white silk weaving seamlessly
into the speckled cloudscapes of piazza san marco's sky
how she awoke like a maiden from a reverie
with blue light caressing her, stone cold pavement not yet trod on
hair as wilde as the dawn fire flames and baby blues iced to cut
both ways
how we exchanged a breath, pretending to know each other in a
reality suspended
on floating prows and a rialto heaving with the weight of faces worn
but not exactly as they seemed
and became everything we wanted to be (together)
despite everything we weren't (alone)
floating on the backs of marble-winged sparrows, no less
entangled in sospiri's sighs than in the blissful slivers of our own
blissful lies, the fluorescent twilight fast dissolving the short-lived
charade,
the thousand other footsteps slowly starting to wake…

> -   *dawn lit the morning like a breath between realities;*

> *like an elongated déjà vu...*

santa maria novella (florence)...

there was an apothecary behind a rose garden in plain sight, hiding. an elixir awaiting to take me to dreaming. when i woke, i found myself in fields of purple, surrounded by bodies that holy hands had sculpted. summer had fast faded, draining every last aquarelle bloodstain from the pastel sky. october vines and blue-veined marble warmed now only by curious gazes; distant memories carved of alabaster, eyes that crave caresses true and soft to the touch just like us; of flesh and bone. scattered, just out of their marmoreal reach among famed red domes where bells hang from brass thrones, an illusion, ethereal. adorned with crowns of sun, light laying tender on the wide open sky, the horizon like an echo between every lost place and time...

ii. grief...

is it possible to go back without feeling? to reflect on an emptiness as elusive as the possessed peaks of hallasan, or as thirsty as every square mile of the gobi that the eye can see? a vastness almost unimaginable unless you've walked every barren inch with your own two feet.

almost...

it's cold that creeps in your bones unsuspected days before you feel it on raised skin. the fool's cloak you put on willingly, now a dizzying haze, a cold dirty numbness, an unsatisfiable hunger but no taste on the tongue. betrayed by the glow you thought you once knew, spinning you round now, wildly, way before you're ready. laser beam memory wiped and question after question thrown on stains that can already, never be scrubbed clean.

all that remains spills like contents from the ribbed suitcase you sit on while trying to force the zippers shut. already losing the race to catch up. it's an entrapment so freeing, and yet, a found peace, immediately lost. in the many, windswept wastelands and oceans left to cross. in the tectonic ricochets of shock.

the "where to next" now caked with bitterness, but persisting, nevertheless.

so, where to next?

seoul...

no one told me how bugaksan bites
i still have the scar on my cheek to prove it. like
the plastic ones smiling down from billboard city
is a new face the supposed token of a life well lived? sorry for the
shade
the sun set on a moon lit afternoon, so it's all a blur
somehow, the getting there, the being there, the endless doing
like when you realise you had a finger over the lens
the entire time icy winds insisted on their taunting
tempos to add to every layer of merino thermal and non. negotiable.
numbness.
meaningless, really, against the deafening howl already pinballing
around the arcades of g-plex.
and my expressionless

exterior.

senses exploded.

time floated.

the leftovers of a life rained down on myeongdong in slow motion
like confetti
playedback 360 in case you missed it, the first time
catatonic and yet, unbothered
by the madness
because it held me. without asking why

- death doesn't play fair

when nerve endings short circuit, you're hardly bothered by raw flesh
preserved, or arabesque eaves that may, at any moment, cave under
the weight, of a fog lit sky. it's more the little things. the islands
shaped like crescent moons, barren, where there should be blooms,
gnawing on the leftovers now scattered at your feet. beauty unseen,
that can no longer be, remedied.

-     namiseom...

hometown glory (banja luka)...

the luna park of my youth sits on lavender, not emerald
and i sit weeping at its leering gate
for the soul of a city they say can never be known
if it was never felt
for the birthplace of my endless transience

tree lined streets once swarmed by lovers lay bare
in the echoes of their own bygone laughter
senses enthralled with the sweet flesh of chestnut
scatter a stripped riverbank embedded with flesh
of a different kind

for every gone glimmer of our untamed beloved
naked feet bathe in a river of blood, instead
home truths exposed this city in tatters
and i sat weeping at the feet of its kastel gate;
an alternate realm of grey skies and sadness

i'm sorry that my youth dismissed such sorrow
and that my memories are made up
or stolen or borrowed
that the only vrbas i know flows from the eyes of my parents
and that it'll never know my reflection nor i, its secrets

i think i know now why my mama loves green
and why i crave another who knows the loss of land and tongue
and why i crave for the pride of those old glory days when pain
was nothing but a reminder of being alive and united
under a sun which barely rises, now

i think i know now why the punchlines expired
souls within souls left in heaps on the floor
of every apartment, no space in the suitcase, next to the fake name
for your friends smiles or your children's lullabies
for your youth fading, passing you by

the old dreamers long gone, their dreams long lost
in glazed eyes scarred with furrow, breaths still not taken
and a river that now only sings a song of sorrow
a still, broken earth from which we still try to rise
falling each time and wondering, why

the rain continues its song of red
dripping into the cracks of a moonscape etched
with the nameless and faceless and their force-handed vows
to never return
to all that remains of their once beloved hometown

- *people question why i don't wear my experience*
like a badge of honour;
it's hard to understand unless you've lived
a lifetime of its aftermath

27

sincerely, sin city (bangkok)...

i came to bathe

my sorrows in saffron

in those chariot drawn temple dawns

of the most sincere of all

the sin cities

    (or so i thought)

    where morning alms don't lie

    but lay proud on blood soaked petals

    waiting to be collected at the feet of thieves

    floating in the same river tossed

    with both prayers

        and sins

like gasps swallowed from the same porcelain cup

of snake blood-

it's a spired sunset, sleeping ton of gold, kind of peace

but laced with empty promises

> *and lucid dreams*

> *the faintest wails of hope can be heard*

> *in the final look over the shoulder*

> *but it's a smog with only the potential*

>> *to clear...*

a prelude to healing (koh samui)...

mist-drenched midnight
aglow with wild
moon, full like the globe
of the sorcerer conjuring
occasional accents
waves coming
to life like shadow puppets
against the night
crashing and pouring
into depths of black
sand distilling, shimmering
ancestors murmuring
their secrets and warnings
and every colour whirling
from the bottom of the bucket

                                         up.

back.

                                       the way.

all.

                                    wild abandon led
                                      to wild embraces

strange, yet familiar...
nameless and faceless
the cracks of a once
neon pink heart
filled with powdered gold
transformation, alchemised
many times
over, it had already begun
disguised
by the cloak of youthful laughter
at this point, still
just a glimmer reflected
in the iris of the toothless passer by...

iii. death and the maiden...

there comes a time the maiden must choose; to surrender to temptation or to become it. to be swallowed by the darkness or to lurk in it. on roads newly narrowed, but taken, nonetheless. don't be fooled by red lips and porcelain, they carry wariness like a weapon (her own rug to pull). where she used to beg for mercy, she now strikes the match, for it is this glow wrapped around her bones that lights her way. guided by the pounding of her low belly drum, she waltzes on death's graves not in grief, but in celebration. knowing that although he can collect his prized possessions and fill his quota with fleshed talismans, he cannot take the urge to live from the living, the lustrous gem born only from within. where leering eyes don't stand a chance against a thousand luminous pathways unfolding from the navel of darkness like the camino's nine ways and its pilgrims dressed in velvet with their new found vision; the antidote to cynicism. so as vivid flames arise and blackened ashes fall, the embers of every ending become the jewelled seeds of every beginning. it may have taken two to tarantella, but this dance with destiny is a decisive solitude, and it goes on. may she always trust enough to lead and to follow.

the merciless tales of ulia...

true to the sun, she enjoys endless beginnings
so she struck her own match
and became
the fire;

melted sweetly
like the single bead of sweat rolling
perfectly down the razor steep cheek
of the flamenco dancer burning
down the cellars of sevilla

dissolved
like the acid tears of angels
filling fountains awaiting
fruitful gifts at the feet
of titans in recline

permeated in crystal
ceilings caving in
on a thousand steps up guarded stairways
all for a single prayer
to be pure again

on shores that glitter
with crystallized turquoise
where midnight misdemeanours turn to dust

by morning

and only scattered ashes remain
mourned by weeping faces;
every grotesque creature carved
of ceramic

relics, of a girl on fire
whose foam-lipped whispers trace
the ocean trails of ulia, now
telling the most merciless tales
there are to be told...

sundays are for lingering (vienna)...

sundays are for lingering
in the shadows of albertina
her coolest corners like balm to soothe
the burn of never ending nights

sundays are for lingering
at the table in the back
above the rings of cigarette smoke
night after night in the same broken throne
made entirely of red

sundays are for lingering
in thirsts unquenched by burnt melanges
and games where red lips are ruled
kryptonite, for black eyed strangers

sundays are for lingering
in eyes that lock like lips
and words that flow like milk
as they try to decipher the longing
of just one, golden kiss

sundays are for thanking
strangers in the street
who stop to tell you not to walk looking at your feet

(in case you're reading this, kind stranger,
it was a while yet, before i believed)

sundays are for lingering
in the shadows of albertina
her coolest corners like balm to soothe
the burn of never ending nights...

the daisy and the lion (delos)...

the curse of delos
is the yellow daisy picked
from the mouth of a lion
by the one who thinks
the heat of the sun
and the cool of the moon
don't coexist

-

be the daisy and the lion

the snake charmer of chania...

the air seemed charged when we left the apartment;
a strangely heightened, electrified current. it had been a long day of
dragging our aching bones through the shadowed valley where giants
sleep, tumbling and spilling from mountains smooth like milk and
pearl and crème, graceful like a song and a dance, cool against our
burning hot skin.

the moon glowed a perfect half; the most luminous i'd ever seen it,
piercing our pupils as we meandered through this confusion of an
old, new, town.

she disgusted and intrigued me all at once standing there in her
jeans and flip flops, casually stroking the dormant python wrapped
around her neck like a louis vuitton or a scaly shawl of some kind,
unenthusiastic in her hustling of every other passer by. i couldn't
tear my eyes away...

in the darkest corner of the port sat a child, of no more than ten.
possessed, it would seem, with a song surely passed down to her
from ancestors and elders both dead and living. she wailed its
shakey melody high into the night, rattling my bones like the
dormant bells and tambourines her tiny hands invoked as they beat
the leathery skin of a worn down drum.

how many peculiarities does it take for coincidence to fade? for the
mystic thread always weaving to reveal itself? i reflected, as minoa
beckoned with her arms outstretched and her hands adorned with
snake-like figures and the blood of men.
was i hypnotised, or awoken?

47

*i couldn't be sure. who was i before i came here, or better yet, when
i came here last? who am i now, that i've seen her again?*

iv. planting seeds...

in search of soil as brave and golden, as any morning promise made by a seven spired catalonian sunrise, i stopped and started a thousand times. on an urban wilderness that unravelled me, like a needle pointing to the clarity, already found within the deepest depths of my own seven seas. the type of wild that points you north, awaiting patiently in the folds of death's cocoon, as you rise in time like haydn's last, through the reputable gloom. like some gloriously rare, concrete jungle bloom. even taller than the tallest shard of glass that rules this kingdom of unruly skies and restless hearts. it was a reflective stillness like i'd never known. the eye of the most perfect storm. so i met myself there, and called it home.

when i left my intuition
was as sharp as the knife
in the fireplace i slept in
the very first night...

-

intuition is a muscle (london)...

great titchfield st...

winter's final whispers faded, as spring unveiled its opening act. i tried to decipher where the cracks in the stark white pavement ended, and where the sky began. not a sound abounded the strangely peakless hour, bar the palpable echoes of my metronome footsteps on great titchfield st. a rhythm that suggested i had somewhere else to be, other than right here. it was another arrival in the endless search, for everything you can think of that's too elusive for words. a knowing unseen, found here first; in the unassuming quiet of the noisiest place. not in a globe upturned like a handbag search of the glossiest lakes or most deciduous leaves. of ever-eroding shorelines, remotely ancient waysides or earliest start times to those extravagantly conquered peaks. of cavernous night skies, novelty sized baja cacti, every filigreed palace or valley full of fairy chimneys forged of timely earth, water, fire and wind. or even the pebbled underside covering the stitched up earth beneath my feet. just right here, as far as the eye could see. to a breath so pure, it had no befores or afters. time with no meaning, nor definite reason. a moment, not particular, but that i remember. looking up blindly to inhale the sun as it trickled slowly down all over plain old london town like honey, down my throat transforming slowly into sweet gold elixir to fill every restless hollow awaiting, still. cause wherever you go, there you come, and go. eyes long open but can they actually see? the blank pages always in your palms, the petalled pathways always at your feet? scintillating as the shimmer of distant mirages may be, it's the glow of presence that comes around like a recurring theme. could this be the clue to pause, and plant the seed?

i used to knock on mountains
as if they were doors
to places i didn't belong
but was desperate for
some reason i made the
vow on soundless green
like the three drops of blood
that pooled perfectly

-

st bartholomä (königssee)...

there's a sweetness in the port (split)...

there's a sweetness in the port
i can't explain or convince;
the cheap plastic burns
and the espresso is bitter
and the ships hum and haw
all day impatient in the distance
hitched rides, sweaty thighs,
unmet promises that linger...
it's a specific kind of sweetness
i just can't explain or convince;

the city that made me (london)...

my favourite time is morning;
when you taste like possibility and possibly glaze
coating all that's left of last night's wandering tongues
when the mischievous sun deliberates, to love or not to love
your river for the day
the infamous pacemaker suspiciously quiet for a sunday
i'll take raucousness on ice and time turned to dust
any day on your spiritual summit
where the spiritual sun sits surrounded by everything
and everyone clad in leopard print bags filled with spirits of the
starving
artist's souls they feast on to trade for jewels
cutting names in lights and crowns in pockets
hearts so callous they bring tales of love
but leave the real thing double bolted, just in case
every walk of life walks the same
edge here; a never ending queue to smoke and mirror nights
that refuse your honey
coated fears sown in soil so deep fruitful blooms shoot
like an acid burn or a brain freeze
or a blaze-through the castle you built with the bricks and bare
hands
you ground to powder
an organised mess on a road of flowers
scattered with fragments of shattered illusion
remnants of who you thought you were

reminders of being lost, but knowing
i am everything because you made me
still

-   thank you

v. love...

distorted memories of a plush warmth radiate long after the lights fade and the seasons change. because a tenderness that shattered tailbones and crowns for miles all around cannot be forgotten. the hope for recurrence still floats among the lilies of giverny, inspiring murky waters with tales of celebration to be immortalised on canvas by gods among men. we all deserve to stand in its presence at least once, after all. especially when wistful dreams of what it could've been are night after night disturbed by the stark reality of what it was. and what it will inevitably remain, until the day we finally stop searching the bottom of tea cups, or hotel rooms, or the panoramic sparkle of montmartre, or every other corner of the tangible earth for an intangibility that ultimately lies dormant within. it took a few, strangely serendipitous encounters for this reminder to stain, like the bordeaux red you hope will give you courage to soak the leftovers of your own life in. just like every city of love already does in its own snoozing sun. accompanied by accordion tunes, no less. the courage to find all of the qualities you'd already attributed to attachment and shine them bravely in the completely opposite direction. for in true love lies a radical freedom. and that is the sweetest ruse of them all.

remember when
instead of relentlessly trying to fuck you
they would tell you your voice was gently melodic
tapering softly at the end of every sentence
like a musical phrase
and you would run through the smoke and the beer haze
of quartier latin
to the closest bar with a piano
simply to see if you could prove their theory...

- those were the days...

paris:

i. the first time

the first time was the greatest...

ii. on fire...

accompanied by tapestries
of florals
silk blouses
felt hats
red lips
and a backdrop
of lily pads
and pink houses,
i burnt a path
through endless rues
of saint-germain
spoken to by strangers
as if they already knew me
by name

iii. in love...

our limbs entangled
in a garden of white
awakened each morning
by billowing curtains
and sunkissed eyelashes

our tongues collected
rogue pastry crumbs
from the corners
of each other's
mouths

as we got lost
with no care
to ever be found...

iv. in my dreams...

an ongoing soundtrack would play
one that we could dance to,
slowly,
in the rain
while people watched on
from cafes
on street corners
we'd sway
float above the seine,
bodies melting
into one another
time, would slip away...
drunk,
on the liquid
pouring, from your mouth
into mine,
the sun
and the moon
would turn three times
and we'd still be dancing...

eden (oxford botanic garden)...

in the garden of eden
october rains blessed
our new beginning
so easily

me,
in a black and white striped dress
you,
with your shirt buttoned all the way up
huddled
under the cheap red umbrella we bought at paddington station
lost
in each other
slow
in tracing the herbaceous border

the canopies had to shed
so that the daffodils could bloom
our skin had to brush
so that the daisy chorus could sing
the dawn redwoods aflame had to foreshadow the start
so that we could reach
our inevitable
end

vi. crumbling...

to crumble is to break. to fall apart. to deteriorate. but only in the longest, slowest way, down. it's running back and forth as the backdrop changes, from hundred year old speckled seasides strung in fives, to sunset pouring on the dumbo skyline, to those year round homeland vines that take your breath away, knowing that as long as your insides succumb to their own journey of decay, it all remains the same, anyway. a hollowness once filled with gold now festers, in monochrome. as the earth beneath dissipates but only in the longest, slowest way, down. a wily limbo with a bet or two watches on as you surrender to the pull, knowing deep down the only way out is through. even if time won't let you move (yet), there's really no use rebelling.

somewhere between cinque terre and copenhagen...

somewhere between cinque terre and copenhagen

i found the most colourful destination

on a map with no queues

of windswept locks or flowing skirts

or pre-prepared peers over the shoulder

to a glittering glass of prosecco or two

just a queue for one

hours spent waiting to ask the terraces to colour my insides

cause i was tired of being monochrome

gundungurra darug land...

my red earth dream came to life
somehow, in the oiled up azure
sky above the valley
you'd fall to your death for
just to get a better look

at shades of green to match
even the most envious of us
skirting the warm rock i was to lay atop
in a later the depths of me
already knew about

in the end it was the same unease
in careless ankles rolling
down worn down stone
like dancing bones impatient
for cascades rapacious

in every slap reaching
for the sweeping cloudscapes
saving their rains for special occasions
a second time now,

why didn't i think of that?

wise shadowlands scattered with yesterdays
ash and winding branches so grotesque
i want to join their dance, every time
just in time to burn again
maybe tomorrow

is sunburn worth the brush of eucalypt?
is love worth the heart scraped
like rugged sandstone by greedy fingertips?
a pointless search of iridescent earth
for gold that was never ours

to begin with, ignoring every warning
cause we're held, anyway
in the hardest of times
but tread light
and don't ever forget...

-   of land and love (one and the same)

peramangk valley...

twenty-six dances
round a luscious winter sun
twenty-six cups
of red wine and tired love

in the lushest green valley
you've ever rolled down
where lamb clouds frolic
in jus de raisin

and the first cold snap
yields gold leafed vines
to feast drowning eyes
and brittle hearts on

happy
birth
day
to
me

hong kong...

i ran across an alphabet of seas
just to get away from my own rib cage shattering
i stopped for breath under a skyfall ceiling
bearing lanterns, bearing paper prayers
fighting to stay swaying
the invisible breeze, not blowing
gladly choked on the thick black smoke of fragrant harbour; it took
a million dollars' worth
of aquilaria to mask the stench of your lies
did you know our love nearly brought an entire species to extinction,
it was that fucking wild? red, orange, yellow glowed, and i begged
them all to take me
home, one by one.
but a different home
one, where no one knows me
hot, dirty, heavy heat, i scrubbed and scrubbed but couldn't get clean
coz sweet boy that forked-tongue of yours turned salty real quick
-ly, didn't it? remember when you used it to conduct me in a
symphony?
and then you went and tattooed lies all over me? with every kiss?
from the outside in?
did you know our love made me so fucking tired i could barely
breathe?
but still i climbed every peak
cause if i couldn't conquer it, i'd dance with every urban deity
instead
up and down and up again
concrete jungle screamed my name
over and over as if she knew i'd forgotten myself

back with you up on that pedestal
skylines morphed one by one
from sunlit to neon lit, i chased my own tail
trying to catch up
with it and myself, i mourned the sun
but not us
cause you made me see this place and every other
from under water

-     *almost like you planned it*

new york (part one)...

if i could inhale you, you'd be snow white
electrifying
sense defying
gone was sadness
replaced by rebellion and scum
in the crease of my elbow and the nook behind my ear
ravaged sockets all dried up, peaks exchanged, from rocky greens
to fire escapes
hiding iron cast stairwells to take me even higher
and you more giant than when we first met in my dreams
there was no real reason for me to be
there that october, walking your centerless grid by night
central park aglow, drowning, in burnt orange and me aglow,
drowning, in you
but there i was anyway, searching for better truths
than the ones i'd brought with me
the kinds illuminated in flashing lights and standing ovations
ignored by new yorkers navigating your concrete catwalks like
landmines
always running, always out of time
i waited all day and all night
for your blaring horns to fill me like he used to
like the sweetest melody centre stage at carnegie
but it all just left me, empty
so i left empty handed
still hardened, it seemed
by the city, and by love...

vii. interlude...

untitled (a garden park in bruges)…

pages turn and petals slip like whispers from confinement. preserved memories of a summer afternoon spent wearing my favourite denim a-line to the bone, on grass soft and warm under the palm and hip that kept me upright. absentmindedly taunting that coveted fourth clover leaf as the late summer breeze kissed my cheeks and brushed my eyelids. confident in, and comforted by, the nowhere else i had to be. funny things, memories, with their power to keep us enslaved in the past or propel us, unnecessarily armed, into every possible future. to be labelled, filed away and relived incessantly until we finally realise they don't even begin to scratch the surface of our true definition. that the only thing that can is how fully we sink breath, blood, flesh and bone, into the possibility of right now. i tore and tossed that little leaf like a "glove slap in the face" challenge to destiny, a vow renewed to look back on in ten years' time, that i'd always be in charge of writing my own. if only i knew then what i know now. still, there's something peaceful about dehydrated reminiscence... almost like, it did its job right...

a rogue memory of a random pier (brighton, or santa monica

maybe)...

i remember every time
i've walked a boardwalk
to endless blue sweeping
across some ocean or
sea, waving goodbye to
the rotating lights on
the ferris wheel behind
me, as if it really would
miss the weight of me.
the slow fade on the arcade
laughter, the only times i've
ever wished i could walk
on water. luxuriously alone;
the wind a cool shadow
across my lips singing
that ocean siren song…

-    *the seaside's always been calling my name*

(thirty lessons) on the road (to thirty)…

1. *the more grounded you become in your own definition of happiness and success, and the further you grow towards your purpose and truth, the more weeds you will start to notice in the garden around the house that you're building. this period of letting go and healing will not be easy, but the flowers you're left with will be so worth it*

2. *you are not of this body...*

3. *...but you are its only caretaker in this life*

4. *you are a caretaker of planet earth; you own nothing, you are owed nothing*

5. *you will only ever scrape the surface of knowing everything there is to know and should approach knowledge as such*

6. *your heart has an infinite capacity for love, healing and forgiveness*

7. *you don't need anyone to do or say anything in order for you to find that love, healing and forgiveness*

8. it is important to recognise when personal suffering becomes a choice

9. you can only be responsible for your own behaviour

10. healing trauma, your own and generational, is your lifelong responsibility

11. living with infinite love, joy and gratitude is your divine birthright

12. you will, always, love again

13. every single being you come across in this life will be a mirror and a teacher

14. intuition is a super power and a muscle that must be used in order to be strengthened

15. it's ok to decide to disengage with something if it no longer serves you, no matter how hard it may be in the moment, or how others may react

16. treat others with kindness, compassion and empathy while knowing it is never your responsibility to betray your true self in order to make it easier for others to deal with their shame

17. it's ok (more than ok, it's good!) to try, fail, try again, fail again and change your mind about anything, at any time

18. if you consider that everyone is always doing their best in every moment, your perspective will drastically change

19. if you approach situations without expectations, your perspective will drastically change

20. you don't necessarily have to see everything through till "the end", just because. sometimes it's braver and more honourable to admit that you're done, even if it feels like you should "stick it out"

21. no relationship is black and white, or tit for tat. we all have unique love languages that must be learned, listened to and respected

22. there is an immeasurable amount of kindness and comradery in the world. if you allow yourself to trust and trust again, people will really surprise you

23. life literally is energy in motion: you really will get out exactly what you put in

24. you must lose yourself as many times as it takes to find yourself, again

25. no education is complete without the school of life. travel, experience, push boundaries so that you can create boundaries

26. no idea is purely original, and that's ok, as long as it's acknowledged and respected

27. no one living being is of more value than any other living being

28. there are only two types of people on this earth: time cops and time thieves

29. you should never be ashamed to be vulnerable, speak your truth, speak your thoughts, to tell another how you feel, to love what you love, to stand up for what you believe in. deep shame is just a projection of the generational trauma of others

30. there are no endings. only beginnings...

krumme lanke...

honestly, we both meant well. me, coming on a tuesday. you, pretending to glimmer all broad and blue past the outskirts. nothing that should've bothered me did. the soft techno weaving seamlessly in and out of the unnecessarily aggressive summer breeze; old friends just like their mistresses and listeners. the whole green apple i had to surrender to the army of bees on patrol; a talisman for their queen, my only snack for the entire. day. the wheezing branch creaking under the weight of the noose like rope from which swung a pack of teenage boys hungry for the furthest, most disruptive explosion of your murky surface. the senseless swell growing on my left calcaneus. the floating cigarette butts and shards of glass deterring my toes from their yearned for dip. the lack of water to swim in and to drink. the careless naked bodies gyrating through space like we weren't about to ride the second wave of a pandemic. the stainless steel buoy, reminiscent of some fly away bunker scrap, taunting me from a distance; a reminder that you can ride to the end of any line but you'll still end up exactly where you started. the ugliness follows you around a bit, in this city. like the bad smell that lingered in the damp brown bank i laid on. the coolness felt nice on my back though...

viii. healing…

eras of heat rise between every layer of land and bone. the air is dense with the smell of rain that lingers in the eyes and the skies finally shedding the waters they once thought they had to cross. every inaudible gasp swallowed, clearly visible now, in the cracks of asymmetry dividing an earth basking in the final fast forward of light. the first road to healing is always the longest and most unbearable. our skirting of its preludes for the longest while, understandable. but eventually we are led back to the self we abandoned at the same floating edge we didn't, and don't want to face, until it faces us, again, and again. waiting for a crystal clear sign to be certain our reflection is one and the same, (spoiler, it is). with a few, hesitant, single digit dips, we prepare our supple form for the grand, fourth digit twist. celebrating every little win with a sip of the salted tears we keep on ice; glacial reminders of the glass half full of hope and the other half emptied of goodbyes. begging the same endings that tore us to pieces and watched on as our cellulose fibres faded slowly into the distance to heal us now, like we've always known that they could. currents may fluctuate, but the underlying pulse beneath, beyond and within remains, always the same. it's peace in a perceived stillness, because stillness does not exist. only the trust in letting go, only the surrender to flow...

water of the spirits (minnewanka)...

the incandescent spotlight

        shone on no one

the lake a sudden portal

        to the spirit realm

or a flow state

        mirror reflected

in a cloud, blinding

        white on rippling

blue gently mocked

        my never ending search

for stillness

        because stillness does not exist

in a place where the sun

        and the moon

are two

        parts of a whole

and the water drips

        water on the carpet

of clouds in reverse

        and the mountains sit in rounds

like wisemen, listening;

        a silent answer

for every silent question

plain of the six glaciers...

single file
mind the horse shit
lake louise like a cup of blue
frozen yoghurt

      getting smaller

         and smaller

   tiny flowers sprayed on

        purple mountains choking on

            people
    straight lined trees like you've never seen,

   a wilderness wilder than your wildest dreams

      walked all day

         step

      by

     step

    all three thousand metres up and i can't

    remember what was heavier

my pack

or my heart

or all six glaciers slowly falling

apart

at our hands

o

n

e

b

y

o

n

e

i saw myself in every creature
in every echo of every feeling i'd ever felt
and every tear these eyes have shed that fell again as blisters bled
we reached an end.

after what seemed forever
head to toe in dust and ember
gasping for breath, desperate for slumber
sordid goodbye happened under cover

of lies, the beginning, a repeat offence
the start of healing, a constant end
just waiting for us to let it hurt
and when we did, boy did it
so. good.

australia day...

when i think of australia, i think of a land that has been hand in hand in a delicate dance for over 65,000 years with one of the oldest and wisest peoples this earth has ever known

i think of their blood spilt, as they fought bravely to guard and to guide her from the greedy hands who sought to possess her no matter the cost, still lingering in the warm red earth that cradles me in my dreams

when i think of australia, i think of the laughter of children now voiceless, their spirits broken, their futures forever stolen

i think of soil that put aside its suffering to welcome with open arms a young family fleeing war, gifting them the seeds to plant and the wisdom to start again

when i think of australia, i think of 65,000 years' worth of subdued wisdom made to watch on, while countless others find freedom to practice their own, as if the sting of every flesh wound didn't run deep enough, already

i think of cultures and languages and stories i wish so badly i had
had to drink, instead of the white washed scraps my white washed
schools threw my way and labelled "multicultural" and "history"

when i think of australia, i dream. of healing elixirs and pristine
waters that catch every single one of my sorrows as they pour from
the places they seem to hang on to. salt turned sweet that flows
from the earth straight into the rivers of my blood. all the way
until we become one.

yesterday, today, tomorrow, i stand with the indigenous people
of my beloved homeland.
elders past, present and future,
who's guidance i still listen for

i yearn with them
i mourn with them

remembering a land that always was
and always will be
theirs

- *an ode to survival*

the bogey hole (an old friend on gadigal land)...

a hundred year old friend holds me, so softly

reunited everytime like lovers;

a hundred warm tongues lick every inch of my body

all at once, weaving infinities

skin is caked with desiccated tears

unforgiven by a sun who knows no other

trajectory but its own

so never with more than i can take or need,

i float

till every salt wound turns sweet

eventually

- *hey old friend*

the great ocean road (gunditjmara, wathaurong, eastern maar,

gadubanud lands)...

it's never too late to find grace. whether it be in the simplicity of a sorry, or the stopping to smell a roadside flower, or the rain. every moment is a chance to stop and start again. no matter what's past, to let it go. for it to be at the same time the end and the start of the longest winding road. where days turn to nights and nights back to days, and we can rejoice in the going of our separate ways. it's ok, for the heart to shatter. to cry. for every piece of what's been to become a vivid, starry night sky that guides you, and me, when all hope seems lost. it's not, ever too late to find your way back, or forward, whichever you choose, just let it be the heart that guides you, there's nothing left to lose.

forgiveness (mykonos)...

it required an audience

seated at tables an ironic peace finger width apart

it required yet another sunset

on a stage, serenading the welling gaze of my mother

it required a slow motion replay

every crack magnified, a long-caged beast escaping

it required a compassion

i never thought humanly possible

and the letting go

of a better past never to be lived

it required willing

water from a stone in a desert surrounded by water

it required a nonlinear mercy

of sorts

- *forgiveness sets <u>you</u> free*

new york (part two)...

still a rebel, but

somewhat softened

by an elevated greenway

and a clarity behind the fog

by waterways veiled

with rage the first time

by second chances and forgiveness

by the city, and by love...

ix. fork in the road…

the swell surged long before the relief kicked in. like a trapped flow finally crashing half moon bay, or heat rising, waiting to hit the epicentre before spreading, or a popped pill, still reeling. i traced coasts, lost in a reverie. stranger to the company i kept, trying to reflect the innermost with the outermost. up and down and round i went, skirting every possible outskirt again. and again. on the road to meet up with an old friend, named intuition. she'd been travelling the insides and we just kept missing, each other. finally, in the same time and place, we came face to face with unavoidable decisions demanding to be made. i had taken as many straight lined roads as it took to avoid turning into stone, waiting for that very last moment to cut the wire. directions cut the thickness now, like a crystalline melody cascading down my rippling heartstrings. a new road was chosen. and this time, i let fate steer.

muir woods (marin county)...

i stood in a forest of foretold memories, an empty, broken, shell of myself. we may have arrived in another time, and to a different place, but there we were again; back with the redwoods aflame, almost ready to fulfil their prophecy. the aged bark soft and cool, with long-limbed crowns, even older and wiser this time round. i made myself small. crawled inside each cracked trunk womb making my way ceremonially up and down that cali coast, from one tree to the next and back again. not to collect souvenirs or coincidental moments to add to a grid of memories but because i wanted to disappear. i needed to disappear. to go so far inward that no one would ever be able to find me until i found me. it took a forest of age-old trees of two hundred and fifty feet to bring me to my knees and accept the damage i'd done to myself, by allowing you to damage me. it was the canopies and leaves i couldn't even see, the ones i would have had to detach my head from my body and throw blindly in the air like a kid playing catch to find that resuscitated me. and if that ain't faith i don't know what is. i drank every sigh and sign spilling from above, feeling, for the first time in what felt like three lifetimes; relief. it was (nearly) the end of the road...

-   *the redwoods know all*

trail of fire (somewhere between fira and oia)...

rugged narrow, dirt road path
lit half in sunrise, half in dark
winding red earth misaligned
morning moon: a warning sign
rare blooms hiding in plain sight
did they already know we were out of time?
days, turned to months, turned to years, hearts grew cold
how many textures can one eye behold?
two steps forward, a hundred back
all the while, the jewel sea glittered,
the bells of oia rang on in the distance...
the sun grew steady and we too found our peak
stone white, bright light, but still,
our cracked lips had no words left
to speak. so we filled the gaps
the only way we knew:
with endless espressos
and endless silence

a city and a love in ruins (athens)...

we walked among ancient ruins

built on sacred hilltops

trying to make sense of history and the thirsty love we clung to

the heat of august exposed even the most godly

of geometry

so how could we expect it wouldn't do the same to us,

if not worse?

every crack illuminated

nowhere left to hide

nothing left to say and no desert blooms to sprout

from this arid soil

so we stood in silence

hand in hand, watching rare shadows perform

their perfectly choreographed dances in the spaces between

columns, as the sunset bathed the acropolis golden

just waiting for darkness to set on us

the mountains

and the sea

kolymbithres...

cracked yolk spread, like wildfire. wayward shells cut, fluorescent blue. dawn waves licked, my bare naked feet sinking deep into the burnt red shore, like an untame kitten playing with its morning milk. my shame stood huge and heavy. gut, like a bottomless pit spreading. unworthy in every way next to rock ravaged for two million years by every elemental expression. pummelled endlessly by rain, wind, sand and sea, and still, it stands proud in the opalescence of it's true identity. while i'd let mine slip away, so easily. why hadn't i aspired to be more like lava ascending, or granite crystalizing, i asked soundscapes to lull nereids and sleeping giants awake. the morning tide replied like a mother's healing touch. a sugarcoat to sweep away every unsavoury memory. a sweetness to remain, on the tip of every tongue...

bohinj...

winter morning gifted solitude

as if i deserved it

the air so crisp it burnt

to the touch

mountains stood stoic

echoing folklore

their rugged peaks so crisp

i wanted a taste of their

naked branches framed

pilgrim's paths to prayer

devil's eye drawn to the rogue

of fuchsia; shades to set retinas alight,

a single sign of a new beginning

the lake seemed still

but was quietly moving;

illusion washed over

passed right through me

as i waited to come to terms

with the end of all endings

lost count of my heartbeat

tried hard not to breathe too loudly

this time knowing to ask no questions

but the answers came anyway
in the pine scented air
and crunch beneath my feet
in the knowing that i'd been
here, already
and that everything was
still, exactly
as it was supposed
to be

red earth dream…

for countless nights
my cold feet roamed
a warm red earth
i felt the heat rise
through my bones
and memory
as i spun wildly
locks long, eyes soft,
limbs clad in white
sent red sand flying
through an expansive
blue hour sky. the sun said
there was no such thing as time
in its absence and i took up space
as if i were alone and unafraid
so it had to have been a memory or a dream
of a place, i haven't yet found
of one, i haven't yet been

x. rebirth...

there's a fear in the newness, of getting it wrong, yet again. skin is raw like a newborn's and the heart beats soft, and slow to start. trepidatious in a world that grew and moved on while you looked to the fire, mesmerised, only for a moment, but now it seems you know even less than you did the first time. nothing to reference but the fallen remnants; sheddings flitting through flickering flames, autumn leaves wound with burn, floating through the sun's rays, leftover pieces of a compass in your pocket and every past iteration of yourself sown into the earth that you must now tread. one last caress of old skin careful not to choke or slip as you dance in circles wild and free, like an old dervish saluting the depths of a soaring sky. a freedom in the trail of gold you leave behind; a reminder that there'll be no fading into the backdrop, this time. it's a new found ease lit by moonbeams and moonbeats; a delicate reality. one where aftermaths don't seem so final, and nothing actually means anything unless you assign the meaning first. a transformation met head on, face to face. a worldwide existence traced. a cycle continuing...

berlin:

i. autumn...

in a smoke filled haze
i found the moon
bathed in its light
then swallowed it
whole as it rained down silver
i dressed in velvet
and danced with strangers
on majestic gold carpets made entirely of leaves
quaking like the bodies
gifted to the beat that peeled them open
relentlessly like a lotus at the touch
or the same chord struck
over and over in a darkness so forgiving
a whole other universe can hide
beating on hearts like pulsing drums while
midnight comes
and goes like the shapeshifters tracing
a different kind of wild…

ii. winter...

orange glow lingers
on honey'd tongues still
sliding in their memorised
sweetness slipping
behind eyelids as grey
as the veil that settles
on an old reminiscence
little stone followed me
home from kitroplatia
rolling round my pocket
like a taunting bet for
every pair of vying eyes
tracing fog lit skies
for even the smallest of prizes
still roaring in the distance
telling sordid winter tales
of fire and ice
one version to the east
another to the west-
the only sky i know
where the clouds still bleed

pastel in december

a spectacular borealis

on winter blues even an

amnesiac couldn't forget

pink dusk creeping like that

unnoticed since morning

settled but slipping

away as you try to catch (it)

iced light sliced of cotton

candy grey with an "almost over" glow

even the copper cherubs know

about, so they play on

with all of the pomp

and the circumstance

of any grand

- *winter in berlin*

is like a collectively unspoken agreement
to watch everything crumble, first
and then try to rebuild it

iii. spring...

it seemed apt that my heart
chose this city of dust
to shed the betrayal,
to root so it could rise

saturn had returned
like a long lost love
melting with the ground
for the longest time

the remnants dissolved
into reminders of feeling
horizon like scars
and a new found healing

it was a diy baptism
in tears and april snow
falling as i bled
so that i could bloom (again)

iv. summer...

we felt the heat rise
and gathered in splendour
you, the pied piper, called us to water
by the water we danced
as you conducted our bodies;
the current of our blood, the rhythm of our laughter
we felt the heat rise
with the sweetness of solstice
from your mouth to ours poured a nectar
so golden it melted our skin
and every fear we were holding
straight into the pounding of drums
scattered beneath our disco ball pillar
of every lost night
awaiting to be sorted
by the invisible hands of fate...

irgoli...

rows of christmas trees
shade a sapphire sea
shepherds call
for the day's co op cheese
the terracotta's cool
on my burning hot cheek
watching ants march by
readily
as the linen line danced
in the tender breeze
my heart beat again
steadily
i inhaled, i exhaled
the morning sun
in the mountain spring
found baptism

- it was slow, to start

saudade...

it had been a long time since i'd felt. this way, about a place, or any other, for that matter. it hit me the moment we began the descent, towards earth side swirls and late afternoon light that poured like gravy over bronzen plains and burnt savannahs shimmering like topazes in the distant september sun. clarion reminders, it seemed, that we must continue to lose ourselves, as many times as it takes to find ourselves, again, just as well...

at the foot of moon mountain a soft wind blew, hummed age old secrets right in my ear. implored, i sank deeper into the darkened forest and danced with shadows, even when their cool air started to bite. felt no fear laughing with cork trees, riding twin leering lions, or spiralling into darkness. because for once it was a theme not of loss, but of searching.

with soft breath and cool body, i rose through the heat. ascended the turrets. got lost in their labyrinth of eighteen colours. you see, i had burned, crumbled and halfway healed, already. taken my own breath away, letting the tears flow, freely. filled oceans to the brim with pieces of myself that had ricocheted in every direction, even returned to salvage the remnants. but i hadn't yet scattered them, among the feathered halos of every replicate madonna, for the new me to find. knowing, full well, she'd embark on the same pointless search for unsung songs of what could've been, live looped into faraway skies. for the same whispered warnings of what was, camouflaged against the spreading cracks of every ancient mosaic tile.

eventually, with every pocket emptied, the day began its slow undress. down with the sun as stars illuminated songs spilling out of windows onto cobblestones. songs as old as the city itself, sung by mouths surely born of pure melancholia. reminders of loneliness, of yearning, of skin, melting with skin. just like we had melted. just like i had melted. just like the sky had melted
with the rooftops.

as i walked the port i thought thoughts of sadness and sorrow. felt my soul shake with echoes of fado and techno and i wondered, which smart happenstance had brought me here, to bid every last, pent up farewell on lands where nostalgia rings eternal like manueline myth and the cracked stone of jeronimo? with a smirk of defeat and a last look over the shoulder, i surrendered to the daylight as if i was worthy. let its golden glow engulf and illuminate me. a clarion reminder, it seemed, that we must continue to lose ourselves, as many times as it takes to find ourselves, again, just as well...

rishikesh...

is it strange to write a love letter to somewhere you've never met?

is it possible? is it heard of?

is it strange that i dream of you so vividly that i can't be sure it wasn't yet true?

that i didn't choke with pleasure on your saffron scented air

or bathe daily in your fountains, made entirely of sound?

that i didn't adorn myself with your music, made entirely of colour

or dance with the laughter of your children

or heal with the cry of your mothers?

when i hear talk of walking your holy river bed
154

i feel the moist earth beneath my feet

devotion hiding in tarnished waters

waiting to be found by every famished seeker

when i close my eyes i'm still suspended

by a single prayer sung above mother ganges

when we meet again it won't be an introduction

but a reunion

-   of souls long parted

desert from a dream (maktub)...

sunburnt sand still hot to the touch

swept sun-kissed skin

burnt away doubt

what if the mirage was just that:

                          a reflection

of the soul's desire for love

of the deepest kind

to be free

with the wild winds blowing

all at once

a vast nothingness

and a vast everything

a deep yearning

and a deep knowing,

all is written…

                     -    *an homage to paolo coehlo*

xi. moving on...

i'm figuring it out as i go; how to keep conjuring serpents in time from the most settled of dust like the priestess of minoa before i'm cast aside, like every other "mad woman" before me. i do miss the power of my youth, sometimes, but i couldn't imagine a life not pumped by this kintsugi heart and it's golden-blood, so divine, i'm tempted to rip it right out- a common cause beacon to light the way for all the "mad women" after me. it remains wild in my mind, that after everything, i still fear being both ordinary and way too much, all at once. hollow on the inside with nothing left for anybody to love, and i think we can all relate to that. because it's completely reasonable to know your worth and still feel unworthy. the difference lies in the transience of emotion, you see. if i could give even a scrap of advice it would be not to get so caught up in the healing that you forget the new life, waiting, begging, to be lived. you can dissect the past a hundred times and it would still remain. because whether we stumble through it with eyes tightly shut, or sink slowly into its sweet luxury, our constellation is long signed by the hands of some grand unseen across the velvety night; a path simply destined for us to take. and there's no point trying to play destiny (trust me, i've tried...). so go on, soak for eons on end in your own afterglow. until a sensuality as soft as milk and a wisdom as old as time seep like mist from every pore, and a purpose fuelled by eternal fire pours from both eyes like twin rivers of devotion. and don't ever be sorry...

red vespa dreamboat (roma)...

red vespa dream boat pulled up by the pont
gelato starts dripping so i lick it
off the side of my pinky (adds a salty touch)
how is it possible to love a changing face this much
the same, a hundred times over the only one i know
who filters light through stone
spitting fire like a meteor
shower from the mouths of river angels
cradling my weariness on their winged-stone
steps (thirty thousand and counting)
triple espresso
for breakfast lunch and dinner
but what's more grotesque
the gargoyles
or the gold
or the flash toothed smile that watches pennies fly
over every unlucky shoulder
lucky, in a way
cause the day begins at night here
and fortune awaits the unlucky...

edinburgh…

i stood on calton hill, watching strange birds float above coal stained palaces like paper planes weaving in, and out, of dark november storm clouds. summers on stages and pacts made to stay strangers otherwise rose to the surface like debris, floating in the sea of glittering streets named for princes and forgotten dreams below. bare white branches framed bare white mountains. stripped me bare as i straddled highlands and lowlands. bathing in the warmth of blood soaked skin, every thistle sting returned, for every heart broken. i chased that winter sunset, up every mud-walled mountain. like the ice cold air could awaken the numbness, and those otherwise dreams weren't crystalized outcasts. like there was hope for the end, of never ending darkness, and the fast melting sun could somehow alight all the unsaid left between us.

- *closure is not essential to your healing*

morning pilgrim (sarajevo)...

morning pilgrim sat on a hill
on the day of rebirth of this city of suffering
still, inside the prison of its own becoming
cause how do you rebuild on a foundation of death
while every turned cheek denies the crush of bone
still, beneath every step
while tears and blood still run as warm and as free
as the rivers afloat with the nameless and faceless
and black ravens roam still searching for flesh
cause no amount of polished stone can mask a stench
so rotten
the hills can't lie
with their panoramas of marble
inscribed with sanguine as deep
as the most scarred survivor, we go on
but the hills that surround us bleed
still, weep
still, remember
still

-   remembrance day

the cretan chronicles:

salt crusted pedicures

and pebbles like freckles

- *kitroplatia, 4:53pm…*

there's something about a sunrise

same same but different

every time

-    *ammoudi, 7:01am...*

how can i stay on this diet

when the sight of you tastes

so. damn. good.

maybe i can get by

licking the salt off my skin

while i swim and pretending

it's you, i'll savour it

one salivating sip at a time

like a sweet cretan wine

i'll pretend that you're mine

- *marmara, 1:13pm...*

rooftops adorned

with majestic midnights

the fight on the street

while i was trying to sleep

the desperation, the longing

the what could have been

-    *rethymno, all hours of the night...*

i don't want to think

in specifics

i want to think

in metaphors

that i can wrap around you

with my tongue

- *hiking thoughts (samariá)...*

pillow thoughts (heraklion)...

how uniquely and effortlessly beautiful cretan women are: graceful and poised with a sharpness to the brow, a toughness to the skin and a hardness to the bone that can only be learnt by a body born of such rugged terrain. a place where carmine lips and manicured fingertips certainly don't belong

how during the day, zeus' homelands look like faraway holograms stencilled onto a clear cut sky
and during the night, young and old gather exactly where the ocean is the blackest; between the glittering mountains and the towering fortress of the neighbouring town, as if they specifically meant to sit and stare out toward nothing

how you think they don't want to, but it's hard for them too, my eyes can be wide and much less than inviting. and why it always takes a faraway stranger to remind me of how bright i shine, like that 3:00 am phoenix sky

how i crave a vodka tonic as sharp as the obsidian blade that sliced my lip, like last night's lover's kiss. how i'm tired and restless but unable to go home because i'm a very good friend (i should really win a prize for that)

*how lilith pounds like a broken record on my low belly drum, the
endless sound of the ocean moving in time to the rising moon, how
i must trust the most, exactly in these moments i don't want to*

*how as much as i try, it's hard for me to sit alone like i used to
love. so many thoughts for this old, new, town of a place. "sit up
straight" my mother said. "don't be afraid of your best assets". so
i walk tall now, swaying my hips like the stray cats of the
heraklion night. savouring every lick of the melting pistachio
gelato running down my wrist. enjoying the breeze blowing
through the gap between my cropped shirt and sunburnt skin...*

xii. covid-19...

inhale   exhale   bones heavy, but, at the same time, floating.
inhale   exhale   skin melting, but, at the same time, expanding.
inhale   exhale   body confined, in spaces, fears and times, both
internal and external. both familiar and not. days become nights
and nights begin to bleed, towards distant tomorrows. every place
and other, your limbs have swallowed, unravel now, layer by layer.
spill into earth, glistening, shining, a dark ruby red. inhale
exhale   cracks spread on arid lips, fingertips trace sanguine love
notes etched in the carpet. tattooed tissue, cellophane crisp, memories
wrap bones, one. by one. remnants to sink (cold teeth) into. inhale
exhale   deafening rush. of fresh blood, so fast, limbs can hardly
keep, up. but they always catch, up. effervescent in the beginning,
transient by the end. inhale   exhale   infinite roadmap,
transcends time. pathways brew, boil, burn, mould, mourn. flesh,
just as before, but, from the inside, now. don't you realise, it's so
very different. but also the same. inhale   exhale   in a single
breath, i am everyone and everything and everywhere, i have ever
seen... heard... touched... smelled... tasted... crumbling decay,
dripping sweat. all the pieces connected, still, by every tip reaching,
anyway, to the ends of THEIR *realities. eyelids thick- veiled*
terrors or kaleidoscope lights. you decide. exhale (darkness)
inhale (light)...

- based on "a movement meditation to transcend ((any)

reality)..."[1]

---

[1] *originally commissioned for dancehouse diaries issue #12.1: what now? -
interior lives*

the world is on hold

but i travel in my dreams

to graze the petals

with my fingertips

\-

nakaragi...

lucky dip trip (covid-19)...

i had planned on celebrating
thirty spins
with a lucky dip trip

to make love to a stranger
in a bedouin desert

or dance barefoot, singing
through a lavender field

instead, i got the house ready
for the main event: fear

adorned my body with garlands
adorned its walls with gold

aren't you sacred, they all asked me
no, i answered;

i've seen death already
i welcome him

secret spring (lockdown)...

dawnbreak...
loss and hope burgeon
ornaments of darkened soil
hints of equal light

whispers...
orchid shadows slip
between cracks, tenacious clay
confinement to crest

offerings...
heat in morning mist
sage smoke tracing song and prayer
shapes of morning fruit

rebirth...
manifestation
so eager snow came again
portal to rapture

sylt...

even before the train slid
down the last stretch
of paper thin
horizon

my fingertips ran
through dried oat flower
wild wind ran
through my tangled hair
(i liked it)

baby daisies danced
in perfect spirals
for the silver sand shining
a thousand silver suns;

tainted,

but nature can't take sides

flying, sand whips us raw

the same, dunes strip us down

to the same. bare. bone.

             -    *the first smell of salt after a long confinement*

prenzlauer berg:

i. oderberger on fire…

pink flames seem to flick their own fragile wounds
as i stare straight down the barrel
to tram tracks burning and melting fuchsia
and falsehood glittering in the distance
but when you arrive it's nothing
but filthy, but oh fucking my
those oderberger skies
set wide eyed retinas alight
every summered twilight
birds caress their shades of sweetness
straight from heaven
with their feathered wing
spans got me wrapped
in candy cane kissed cheeks
and ultra violet eyelids
wishing hard on every pair of blues
that passed me by
every sunset past
you got me
good

ii. zionskirche...

the eye of the storm
the androgynous mountain i sit on
the piercing shriek of trams turning the radial corner
like nails on a chalkboard
cuts deep
round and round i go
noise fades
silence calls

curse of the maverick (chorin)...

i never truly knew homesick

until i felt it in the deepest

pit of my belly, that place

where shame usually lives

now burns with a yearning

for a long awaited immersion

in the holiest waters

of my beloved homeland

but my place isn't there

this time round or yet again

it's with the teeth in my mouth

and the leaves at my feet

as they converse and bleed

steadfastly

xiii. there are no endings. only beginnings...

what can be said for endless turns, of sapphire suns and opaline moons? for journeys on end through phenomenal foliage, on earth that crumbled, through skies that opened? anything i think of seems arbitrary in the face of such impermanence, so how then, to signify that which continues to begin? maybe with the lack of fear, or doubt, or shame, left in the knowing. with a transient shift from doing to being. from chasing to allowing as you meet your true self, smack bang in the middle, somewhere. shaken and shaken and shaken by fate, all the way until your bones and essence separate. consider this a pause, a momentary drip of silence. a sweet drizzle of quiet to soak in, before the new song begins...

island home (djubuguli)...

i close my eyes and in a moment flawless

waters inhale my endless flaws,

without question or thought

memories afloat, the dreaming

once lost now whispers sent

with the wind

when i'm everywhere

and nowhere, all at once

deafened by silence

suffocated by loneliness

drowning in yearning,

i remain

imprinted by red earth and every merciless

foam-lipped kiss, swaying in time

with my own grazed skin

dressed by grains of gold hiding

in the folds of every fingerprint

and time becoming still

all the way until my blood runs dry

and my bones turn to dust

i remain

- *home*

passing ishtar's lapis gate

took me back to your embrace

both remnants of a long lost

babylon

lost in transit (changi)...

we sit in dim-lit darkness

watching wind-whipped grass flutter

alongside the tarmac

waiting to be herded like cattle to some strange, sleepless place

fumbling through delirium, performing our soft-slumbered dances

to woven soundtracks of sleazy jazz and k pop

our tired limbs and forlorn eyes would trace every spiral

etched in the carpet

in our desperate search for fellow diamonds

to remind us of hope we can't change

where we've come from

nor should we want to

but where we go

next that's ours

for the taking

new york (part three)...

i'm still dancing in the dark

rocking back and forth

craving summers in new york

those warm breeze like fingertips

across my neck like distant chimes

that take me

back to those filthy hot julys

with their roaring fire skies

and smells of yearning in the air

all of the alone-ness but none of the despair

this time round, cause you won't be there

to weigh me down

a reminder so cold

it's distant

but still, reminiscent...

- *i'll never again give myself*

or any place up

to anything
or anyone

postlude…

a note on love

for the loved and the lovers

for the ones deep in it and the ones still skirting

its ever elusive exteriors

riding every breath that roams

even the most stubborn of shallows

coaxing softness

in, and out...

a reminder of the untouchable power

that travels through you

every layer, but a vessel for the intangible

maybe caught fleetingly in the reflective iris of another

or some far away sun beam tracing the ridges of a snowflake

like playful fingertips on the spine of a lover

in the dreamy slivers that evaporate

the moment you wake

sipped like coffee

an internal beat, relentless song

sung on, and on

with a few cracks, perhaps

from the times you abandoned yourself

but remembered to come back

filled with powdered gold

now, but still beating

kintsugi heart

still loving, still forgiving

still whole, nevertheless...

...

About the Author

anja mujic is a Yugoslav / australian dancer, musician, yoga teacher and writer based everywhere and nowhere all at once. after a steady unravelling of words commissioned for various performances, publications and platforms, she now releases her first book; love letters to places..., a decade's worth of memories, dreams, moments and epiphanies exploring a multitude of themes on a simultaneous journey of inner and outer discovery. she invites you deep into the present moment through pasts and futures shaped by loss and grief, love and heartbreak, crumbling, rebuilding, healing, inspiration and the endless possibility for new beginnings...

Acknowledgments

to ian and the entire leschenault press / book reality team for your
guidance, expertise and belief in bringing my work to life,
to annabel zenith and luke buxton for your divine work on the
cover art / design,
to my family and friends for your lifetime of love, encouragement
and support,
to friends, lovers and teachers past, for every lesson,
to every time, place and other i've thus far encountered; it is
because of the clarity in your reflection that the most fleeting of
moments could find themselves so gloriously immortalised within
these pages,
and most of all, to you, dear reader, who cared enough about my
work to reach this point,
i remain forever grateful and in awe…

CPSIA information can be obtained
at www.ICGtesting.com
Printed in the USA
BVHW081846220222
629771BV00004B/315

9 781922 670328